WE'RE DOING WHAT FOR SUMMER VACATION?

WE'RE DOING WHAT FOR SUMMER VACATION?

CINDY DAVIS
AND
ALI ROLLASON

authorHOUSE®

AuthorHouse™
1663 Liberty Drive
Bloomington, IN 47403
www.authorhouse.com
Phone: 1-800-839-8640

Published by AuthorHouse   04/30/2013

ISBN: 978-1-4817-4674-8 (sc)
ISBN: 978-1-4817-4673-1 (hc)
ISBN: 978-1-4817-4734-9 (e)

Library of Congress Control Number: 2013907437

This book is dedicated to Steve and Zak Rollason—our partners in this adventure and in life. The road less traveled is not the easiest path, but it makes for the best journey.

CONTENTS

PREFACE

"Where's Borneo?" That was a question we heard a thousand times before we left on our summer adventure. We soon discovered that Borneo was a unique place that challenged us in ways we never imagined. It was not a relaxing month at the beach. It was hard traveling that required us to all work together as a family. It was a place where we spent our days and nights playing card games and talking about life. It was a place where we learned the real meaning of being poor and hungry. It was a place where we learned about bedbugs and leeches. It was a place where we learned about the Muslim culture. It was a place where we learned the fear of losing a child. It was a place where we learned that a long trek through the jungle led us to the most amazing waterfall we had ever seen. It was a place where we learned to trust and depend on the kindness of strangers to keep us safe and to welcome us into their homes. It was a place where we learned that we could sleep just about anywhere. It was a place where we learned to "just go with it"!

This is the true story of our adventures through the eyes of Ali, a nine-year-old American girl. We are very grateful for the support that we received to make this book a reality. We would like to give a special thanks to our friends in Borneo, Peter and Harni. We are grateful for your assistance. We would also like to thank our family and friends who encouraged us to tell our story and gave us feedback on this book. Thank you, Lisa Carnes, for the daily encouragement to publish this story and keep writing. Thank you, Uncle Andy, for your editorial comments and enthusiasm for this book—it was just what we needed!

Last but not least, none of this would have been possible without Zak and Steve. Thank you for all the adventures and for always watching out for us!

CHAPTER 1

My Not-So-Normal Life

I would like to say that today was just another typical day in my life, but *wrong*. "Typical" just doesn't cover it today. I'm a normal nine-year-old girl named Ali, with a fairly normal twelve-year-old big brother, Zak. We both play soccer and basketball. We assumed that we were going to spend the summer at the lake or going to the beach in Florida with our friends.

Although we are normal kids, I can't really say that our parents are normal. They look like normal parents, but they are really former backpacking hippie people who think we need to see the world and experience unknown "adventures." I think a summer vacation at the beach in Florida is adventurous enough for me! Their hippie life started long before they had my brother and me. They met in some weird place called Tioman Island in Malaysia when they were both backpacking for years in Southeast Asia. My mom is American, and my dad is English. They try to act like ordinary parents, but I know that they are really very different from most of my friends' parents.

Today, I was outside playing on my trampoline, and Zak was playing Xbox in his room when Mom called us into the kitchen for a family meeting. I wondered what was so important that we needed to have a family meeting. These meetings usually mean that we need to talk about something important or make a major family decision. We all gathered around the kitchen table, and Mom announced, "We are going to spend a month in Borneo this summer."

I said, "What? Borneo?"

My brother said, "Where is Borneo?"

Dad explained that Borneo was a big island near Malaysia and Indonesia. Of course, I had no clue where those places were either. They could have told me we were going to the moon because I was clueless. All that I could think about was not getting to play with my friends, go the lake, or go to the beach!

Zak seemed to understand what was happening a bit better, because he had been to Hong Kong several years ago, with Mom. Zak asked, "Will it be like Hong Kong?"

Mom said, "It is the same part of the world, but it will be very different."

Dad laughed and said, "Borneo is where headhunters come from, and the orangutans."

"Great!" I said in my really sarcastic voice.

Mom was so excited and said that it would be a great summer adventure. Zak seemed to be a little bit excited about the trip, but I was not at all looking forward to this so-called adventure! I just wanted to be a normal kid with a normal family. Was that too much to ask for in life?

After realizing that this big adventure was really going to happen, I decided that I needed to find out a little information about this so-called Borneo place. I looked on my globe, but I didn't see any place named Borneo. I found England and Florida (where I really wanted to go this summer). Since the globe didn't help, I thought school was a good place to get some answers.

The next day, I asked my third-grade teacher, Mrs. Miles, if I could go to the library. She said, "Okay," because she loves for us to read books.

I walked down the hall to the library and asked the librarian, "Do you have any books on Borneo?"

She said, "Where's Borneo?" When the librarian doesn't know where a place is, you are in big trouble, because librarians are super smart people and know all the books! I took this as a *very* bad sign.

I soon realized that *nobody* knows where this Borneo place is. Every time I would tell someone that I was going to spend my summer in Borneo, they would say, "Where's Borneo?" I even heard people ask Mom and Dad that same question when they would talk about Borneo. Why in the world do my parents want to take us to someplace that nobody even knows about? Maybe nobody goes to Borneo because of those headhunters that Dad told us about! This was not sounding like a fun trip.

CHAPTER 2

Help! I Have To Get Shots

About a month before we had to leave, Mom told me that we had to do a few things to get ready for our big trip. I instantly thought of shopping! Oh, we would go to the mall and I could get new clothes and new shoes and maybe even a new bathing suit. This sounded like something I was going to love, and I would need lots of stuff for my stay in Borneo. I planned to take lots of new clothes and stuff to last me an entire month!

Unfortunately, shopping was not what Mom had in mind. She announced, "We have to go to a special doctor to get some important shots and malaria pills for our trip."

I said, *"What? Shots?* I don't do shots! I hate shots! Why do I have to get shots to go on this stupid trip?"

Mom tried to explain that she had to get lots of shots when she went to Africa, but this was not making me feel any better. I then asked, "What the heck is malaria?"

Well, apparently it is some very weird disease carried by mosquitoes that can make you really sick and kill you.

Okay, excuse me for asking again, but why are we going to this place no one has heard of with strange diseases and killer mosquitoes? I bet my friends going to the beach in Florida do not have to get shots or worry about killer mosquitoes.

The day we had our appointment at the "travel clinic," my brother and I were both a little cranky. Summer vacation was not supposed to involve shots!

Mom, Zak, and I all went back to talk to the doctor together. He asked who wanted to go first. I said, "I'll go first because I want to get this over *ASAP!*" I had to have two shots—one in each arm. It was a very big needle, and it really did hurt, but not as much I expected.

It was my brother's turn next. Zak asked, "Ali, did it hurt?"

I said, "It was worst pain *ever!*" just to scare him. He hates shots too.

Mom went last and her needles were even bigger than ours. She had to have three shots, but she acted really brave.

The doctor also talked to us about not drinking the water and wearing lots of mosquito spray and staying close to our family. The only good news was that he said that it is fine to drink Coca-Cola out of the bottle. This sounded really great, because my mom almost never lets me have Coca-Cola. Maybe Borneo will be filled with lots of Coca-Cola and other things that I'm not suppose to drink at home.

About a week before we left, Mom told me that I needed to pack for Borneo. She said, "Each of us can only take one small bag, because we will be moving around a lot in Borneo."

I told her, "I can't get clothes for a month in one small bag. I like to wear different color flip flops with all my cool outfits." She also told me to pack one long skirt or dress because Borneo is a Muslim country. I thought that sounded really cool, because I knew they wore the long dresses with scarves around their heads. I wondered if I would need to dress like that in Borneo too. I found a very cute long dress to pack, but I couldn't fit the cute shoes that matched into my bag.

Although we didn't have much room in our bags, Mom said that it was important that we take stuff to help the poor people. We decided to collect soccer jerseys from our soccer teams, because everyone in the world loves to play soccer. Mom told me that I had to stuff as many soccer shirts as possible into my one and only bag. This was not easy, because I wanted to carry my cute flip-flops too. Mom said, "Oh, and don't forget to pack your sleeping bag too."

"*OMG* . . . Are we going to have to camp?" I asked. I was planning on a fancy hotel with those little shampoos and chocolates on my pillow.

CHAPTER 3

The Longest Flight Ever

We finally got all packed and ready to go. The worst part about leaving was saying goodbye to my three dogs: Spike, my little English Bulldog puppy; Malika, my Lab, named after an Aboriginal boy we met when we went to Australia; and Butch, my old Akita dog that watches after me. My grandma was keeping my dogs, because she has two dogs too, and she lives on a lake, on a farm. The dogs love staying with her, but I was really sad to leave them. My dogs looked really sad when I kissed them bye at 6:00 in the morning, but Spike, the bulldog, always has a really sad face, even when he is happy.

We got breakfast at a little market and headed to the airport in Nashville. I hate to fly! I am just not an airplane kind of person. I know why this happened. When I was about five years old, we were skiing in Colorado, and we had to take this little tiny plane back to Denver. It was a really, really snowy day and a snowstorm came through the mountains. It was the worst flight ever! The plane was bouncing up and down, and everyone was getting sick. I was so scared that I starting crying and having a panic attack. I wanted off that plane so bad. The flight attendants even looked scared, and they are supposed to be calm. My parents kept telling me that everything was going to be all right, but I didn't believe them. Parents always say that kind of stuff. When we got off that flight, I decided from that moment on that I hated to fly! I started making a fear list, and flying was on the top of the list!

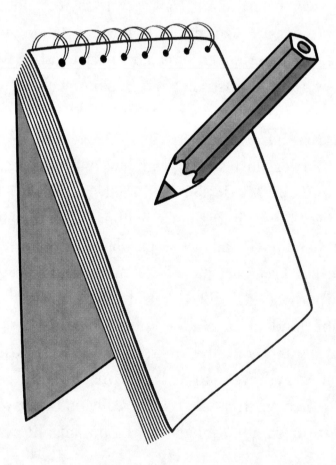

So, needless to say, I was not excited about flying all the way to Borneo. Dad told us that we would be flying for about two days. I said, "We could be at the beach in Florida in just a few hours by driving in the car!" Mom and Dad gave me one of those looks that parents give kids when they are not being very cooperative.

Our first flight was to Los Angeles. I had been to California lots of times, because my Uncle Robbie and Aunt Allison live in San Diego. I love visiting San Diego. I bet it would be more fun to spend a month in San Diego than in Borneo! It was a really long flight to California. It took us nearly five hours to get to California, because we had to stop in Texas. When we arrived in Los Angeles, we had to push all our bags to the international terminal and check into a different terminal. It took a long time to get through security. We had to show our passports and be very serious when going through all the security screenings. The policemen made us take off our shoes and go through this machine that looked like a space ship tunnel. I was so afraid that I would do something wrong and get arrested by the police. When I was standing in the security line, I noticed people talking in all kinds of different languages. I couldn't understand what most of the people were saying. Dad told me that some people were speaking French, some were speaking Spanish, and another group was speaking German.

Being from England, he knows more about languages than the rest of us in the family.

We didn't have very much time to make our flight, but we were all hungry. I told my family that we should go straight to the plane, but they insisted on stopping at a little cafe to get a quick bite to eat. We ate fast and then got to our plane. They should have listened to me, because people were already lining up to board the plane when we got to the gate. As we were standing in line, my mom asked Zak, "Where is your backpack?"

He looked around and said, "I must have left it in the little cafe!" This was really bad news, because his backpack had all his cool stuff, like his iPad, iPhone, and those awesome Dr. Dre Beats headphones that I really want.

Mom said, "I will quickly run back to the café to see if I can find it." I was very nervous, because I just knew that she was going to miss the fight. I was not going to Borneo for a month without my mom! It seemed like forever until she returned, but then I saw her running toward us, carrying Zak's backpack. Wow, that was really lucky!

As soon as Mom got back, we boarded the plane. We were flying on Singapore Airlines, and Dad said that it was one of the nicest airlines in the world. It was the biggest plane that I had ever seen. It had an upstairs area for people to sit, and the really rich people could stay in first class, which had little suites with their own beds. I asked my parents if we could stay in the suites, but they said that it was way too expensive for us. Maybe one day when I get really famous, I will get to stay in one of those suites.

On the plane, we had an entire middle row of four seats for our family. Every seat had its own TV screen and remote control. It was the coolest plane ever! The flight attendants gave us a little bag with a toothbrush, toothpaste, and socks. Before we took off, the flight attendant also gave everyone a very hot washrag. I had no idea what to do with it, but I saw my dad washing his face. I'm not sure why they wanted us to wash our faces with a hot rag before we started the flight, but I just did it anyway. Everybody on the plane was washing their face.

The flight from Los Angeles to Japan was twelve hours. I was very nervous when the plane took off, and I held my mom's hand for good luck. We always hold hands on planes during the takeoff and landing for good luck. If the plane crashes, I definitely want to be holding Mom's hand. Everything seemed to be going fine until I heard a loud banging noise coming from the bottom of the plane. That was it . . . I knew we were going to *crash!* This loud banging continued for about ten minutes. It sounded like the bottom was falling out of the plane. I looked at the flight attendants, and they looked scared too. I knew this was a really bad sign. I started to cry and get very anxious. I looked at Mom and said, "Get me off this plane right now!"

She spoke to me in her "calm voice" and said, "Ali, it will be okay; just try to relax. If something is wrong, they will just turn the plane around and take us back to LA."

"If they turn the plane around, I am *never* getting back on it again," I said. My mom used to be a therapist before she became a professor, so she is really good at using her calm voice and dealing with scared people. Sometimes she tells me to just close my eyes and think about being at the beach or somewhere really fun, but none of that was working this time. I heard a big bang, and I knew we were going to *crash* any minute!

Finally, the pilot came on the loudspeaker and said, "The landing wheels fell down but we have reset the system and everything is now okay."

Well, I was not so sure about that. "If the wheels aren't working right, what the heck is going to happen when we try to land in Japan?" I said. This was not a very good sign. Mom told me not to worry, because the pilot had everything under control. I may only be nine years old, but I know when things are not right!

The rest of the flight was pretty smooth. Luckily, the flight had some of my favorite shows. I watched *Good Luck Charlie*, *Wipeout*, and a few movies to take my mind off worrying about the plane not having any wheels to land on in Japan. They also fed us dinner on the plane and gave us Ben & Jerry's ice cream for dessert. I tried to sleep on the plane, but Zak took up most of the room. He always seems to get the good spot first, and then I had to lay my head on top of him. It was really hard to sleep and get comfortable in the plane seats. It seemed like *forever* until we landed in Japan.

We got off the plane in Japan and just walked around. We only had about an hour before our next flight. I looked in the snack shop, but all the snacks were really weird with strange writing. I did find a little can of sour-cream-and-onion Pringles, so I got that for my snack. I went to the bathroom; Japan has the coolest toilets *ever!* The toilets had all these really cool buttons that looked like a TV remote control. One button shot water up your bottom, one button blow-dried your bottom, and another button spayed deodorant on your bottom. I wish we had these high-tech toilets at our home in America.

Our next flight, to Singapore, was seven hours. We got back in our same seats. The flight attendants brought us another hot rag, so I washed my face again. I still do not get the need for cleaning your face, but it did feel kind of good. I was extremely tired when the plane took off, and I was a little nervous about the plane wheels having problems again. Thank goodness, the plane did fine this time, but I still held my mom's hand for good luck.

Zak and I both fell asleep as soon as the plane took off, but, of course, he had the best spot again. I had to sleep with his feet in my face. There was nothing easy about sleeping on the plane. Mom was so tired that she laid on the floor and slept for a little while. She had to hide so the flight attendants wouldn't see her. Then she switched with Dad, and he got down on the floor. When he tried to get up, he was stuck, and we all had to help him off of the floor. I don't know how the flight attendants didn't see him.

We finally arrived in Singapore at 3:00 a.m. Singapore Airport is the greatest airport in the world! They had Starbucks coffee and Dunkin' Donuts, which were still open. Then we walked around and found the entertainment area. It had a movie theatre, PlayStation games, Xbox Kinect, and computers. Best of all, it was all free! Zak and I were so excited. Zak played Fifa on PlayStation with a man from China, and I watched them. It was very funny because the man from China kept screaming, "Zak, Zak" (which sounded like "Jack, Jack") very loudly and laughing. Then we all went and played on the computers. We played for hours while we waited on our last flight. I could have stayed in that airport forever!

It was finally time for our last flight, from Singapore to Borneo. This flight was only three hours long, and I was very pleased. I had never been on so many planes and in so many airports in my life. When we arrived in Borneo, we went through immigration and showed our passports. Dad and Zak went to one counter, and Mom and I went to another counter.

The lady looked at Mom's passport and then started asking her all kinds of weird questions. Something didn't seem right to me, and then Mom told me to go get in the line with Dad and Zak. I wanted to ask Mom what was happening, but she looked at me and put her finger over her lips and went "*shhh.*" I knew that meant for me to just be quiet and do what she said. I moved over to the line with Dad and Zak. Dad, Zak, and I got our passports stamped and went to the waiting area, but Mom was still talking to the immigration lady. We walked over toward Mom and discovered that the immigration lady did not think that the passport picture was really Mom. After talking for a few more minutes, the lady finally said it was okay for Mom to go into Borneo. I was so happy that they let her come with us.

By the time we finally arrived, we had been traveling for thirty-six hours! That was the longest trip *ever!*

CHAPTER 4

Things Are Different

We got a taxi to go to our hotel in Kota Kinabalu, and the first thing that I noticed was that the steering wheel was on the wrong side of the car! They also drive on the wrong side of the road. This felt so weird to me. Dad was used to this, because they drive on the wrong side of the road in England too. As we drove to our hotel, I looked out the window and saw lots of people walking on the streets. The women were dressed in headscarves, long-sleeved shirts, and long skirts, and the men were dressed in shirts and long pants. It was very noisy with old buses and taxies everywhere, and people shouting and honking. There were lots of old buildings and shops with signs everywhere that we couldn't read.

We got to our place to stay, but it was not one of those big fancy hotels like I was hoping. My parents think that we need to experience the "real" Borneo, so we had an apartment in the city to stay for a little while.

Our apartment was okay but nothing fancy. It didn't have any little shampoos and soaps like you get in the nice hotels or a mini-bar with lots of snacks. It had basic old furniture, two bedrooms, a TV room, and a little kitchen. The kitchen was dingy and seemed a little dirty. This was definitely not like the resort we stayed in last year when we went to the beach for summer vacation.

Mom and Dad said that the first thing we needed to do was to get some Borneo money, because we couldn't use our American money. We walked on the streets to see if we could find a place to change our American money for the local money. It was very hot and humid, and there were lots of dogs just running around in the streets. The dogs were very skinny and looked hungry. They did not look like pets or like they lived with a family. I thought about my dogs at home and how much they would hate living on the streets in Borneo.

The people looked different too. Most of the women were dressed in headscarves, long-sleeved blouses, and pants. I loved looking at all the pretty ways they dressed. Some of the women wore really bright colors, like bright pink or purple, but others wore just plain long dresses and scarves on their heads. Even the little girls my age covered their hair and wore long dresses. It seemed so hot to have on all those clothes. Everyone stared at us because we were the only Western people walking on the streets. I wondered if I was supposed to be dressed like

Muslims too, but Mom said, "It is fine for us to wear our normal clothes because we are not Muslim. Covering up your skin and being modest is part of their religion."

We found a big market with hundreds of little shops, including a money-changer shop. Dad changed some of our American money for Malaysian ringgit (this part of Borneo is part of Malaysia). My dad said that three ringgit were equal to one US dollar. This was going to be very confusing for me. My brother is much better at math than me, so I hoped maybe he could help me figure it all out. The money was much smaller and looked very different. It looked like play money.

We decided to go grocery shopping to get some food. This was an experience! They didn't have any of my favorite snacks. All the food looked really funny, and I couldn't read any of the packages. I was hoping to find some bacon and eggs for breakfast, but Dad explained they didn't sell any pork products in Borneo because eating pork is forbidden in Islam. When we went to the meat section of the store, there was blood on the floor and flies on the meat. Zak and I gagged from the smells and felt sick. There was no way that we were going to eat any of that food. We finally just got some bread and milk, but the milk was even different. It came in a box and was hot! I always thought milk had to be cold and in a plastic jug.

After getting our groceries, we went to the outdoor market, which was like hundreds of tents with little lanes to walk around them. I found some Dr. Dre Beat headphones, just like my brother's, for only a few dollars.

Zak said, "Those are not the *real* Dr. Dre Beats," but I didn't care because they looked just like his, except in pink! Dad said that I could get them, and I was so excited. They only cost a few dollars, and I think they are as good as my brother's!

The outdoor markets also had all kinds of weird food. When we came to the meat and fish section, the smell was *horrible*. There were chickens and fish everywhere. Zak and I gagged at the smell. Mom and Dad explained that this was common in markets, but Zak and I wanted to get away from that part of the market really fast. It was making us sick. My mom is a vegetarian, and she laughed at us and said, "See, you should all be vegetarian like me!" If I had to shop in the market, I think that I would become a vegetarian too.

Zak and I were really hungry but were afraid to eat after seeing the stuff in the market. We saw a McDonalds and both got very excited. We went to get something to eat, but this McDonalds was different from those in America. It didn't have the Mocha Frappe that Zak loves. We ordered a sausage McMuffin, but it tasted really weird. The sausage was not like the American sausage—it was a different color and tasted different. My dad reminded us it was because they do not eat pork in Borneo, so the sausage was different, and they did not have any bacon. I had a feeling that eating for a month in Borneo was going to be a problem, especially for Zak, because he is a difficult eater, even at home. Luckily, I love rice, and there was rice to eat everywhere, even for breakfast!

Other things were different too. When I was walking around the market, I had to go to the bathroom really bad. Mom found a public bathroom, and we went inside. I was expecting a normal toilet or a fancy one like in Japan. But, the toilet was not normal or fancy. It was just a hole in the floor that you stood over. I looked at the toilet and said, "What the heck?"

Mom laughed at me and said, "Those are the normal toilets for Asia. You just squat over the hole like you are going to the bathroom in the woods when we are camping."

Luckily, I was very good at going to the bathroom in the woods! Instead of toilet paper, they had a rubber hose. I wasn't sure what the heck to do with the rubber hose, so I yelled at Mom, "There is no toilet paper—just a hose like to water the plants!"

Mom informed me that I was supposed to use the hose to wash myself when I was done. I said, "Okay, whatever!" There was nothing easy about trying to wash myself with a hose in a bathroom with no towels or toilet paper. Needless to say, I ended up getting my clothes, shoes, and the bathroom soaked! I don't understand how the locals could wash with the hose without getting their clothes and shoes wet. My mom went to the bathroom, and she got wet with the hose too! The rest of the trip, Mom always carried tissues for us in case we had to go to the bathroom, but I got really good at squatting over the funny toilets. I actually kind of liked them!

CHAPTER 5

Bedbugs

The first few days in Borneo were rough, because our days and nights were all mixed up. When it was day in Borneo, it was night in America. We were so tired in the day and then wide awake about 3:00 a.m. Dad said that we were suffering from jet lag. The good news was that the European Cup Soccer was on live at 3:00 in the morning, so our whole family got up and watched the soccer games in the middle of the night.

Our little apartment was sort of dirty, with bugs crawling in the kitchen. My mom left a bowl of cereal on the counter for just a few minutes, and when she went back into the kitchen, little bugs were all in the bowl. The bugs were different from the bugs we have in America. We couldn't see any bugs until we left food out, and then they appeared out of nowhere and attacked our food. I kept checking my food to make sure the bugs had not gotten into it. Mom and Dad decided that it wasn't a good idea to cook in our little kitchen.

After being in the apartment for a few days, Dad began to itch and itch and itch. It looked like he had hundreds of mosquito bites on him. Bug bites were everywhere on his skin, in little rows. No one else was getting bitten by the mosquitoes or bugs except my dad. He did some investigating and figured out that he had been eaten alive by bedbugs!

I said, "What? Bedbugs?" Bedbugs sounded really creepy to me. I did not like the idea of any bug crawling on me at night, especially bugs that bite and cause you to be really itchy. Mom tried to reassure us that every country has bedbugs, but I had never seen bedbugs like this before. I didn't care how common bedbugs were. I just wanted to be in a place that was *bedbug free!*

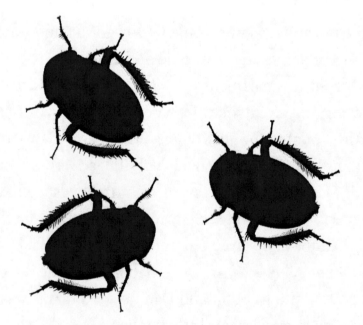

My parents decided that we needed to move from our apartment as soon as possible. I said, "Maybe we should try a really nice hotel instead of living like the locals." My mom gave me one of those looks and said, "This is all part of the adventure!"

I don't know what she was thinking, because bedbugs were definitely not part of *my* plans for the summer. Dad and I went to talk to the owner of the apartment in his little office on the main street of Kota Kinabalu. His office was a small room above a local restaurant. My dad told him about the bedbugs and showed him his arms and legs. The owner felt very bad about our situation and gave us back the money that we had paid for staying at the apartment.

Good news—we were no longer staying in the apartment with bedbugs. Bad news—my parents had no idea where we were going next. Zak and I started packing our bags and checking to make sure that the bedbugs weren't on our stuff, even though we really didn't know what the little insects looked like. Zak kept telling me that bedbugs were crawling on me and in my hair. He always does things like that to scare me!

While we were packing, Mom went to make a few phone calls and tried to find us a place to stay. She is really good at that sort of stuff. We call her our "family travel agent." A few minutes later, Mom came back to the bedbug apartment and announced that we were moving to a place just south of the city, on the coast. No one complained, because we were all just happy to be leaving the bedbugs behind. I didn't even ask if it was going to be one of those fancy hotels with room service and little snacks in the minibar.

It was getting dark and the drive to the new place was going to take about an hour. We were all hungry and tired. We took our bags and found a little Indian restaurant for dinner. Indian food is one of Zak's favorite foods. We all loved the papadoms, the naan bread, and the chicken tikka masala. It tasted like the best food *ever!* We were so hungry that we ate until our stomachs hurt.

After dinner, we got in a taxi and headed to our new place to stay. It was dark and difficult to see where we were going. Zak and I fell sound asleep, cramped on either side of Mom in the back of the tiny taxi, with our bags in our laps. After riding about an hour, we arrived at this little place with a dog sleeping in the doorway. A Malaysian lady, Irene, greeted us and was so sweet. It was late at night, and she could tell that we were very tired. She had been waiting for us to arrive. She showed us down a narrow path to our little room. As we were walking, Zak and I saw lots of geckos on the roof.

Irene gave Dad the key to our room, and he unlocked the door. Our room was small and cozy with two small beds and a mattress on the floor. It was simple, clean, and opened up to a porch that led to the sea. It seemed like paradise after the apartment with bedbugs, but was nothing like a hotel in America.

Zak and I checked under the bed and around the room for bedbugs, but we didn't see anything except a small arrow painted in the corner on the ceiling and a gecko climbing up the wall. Zak and I wondered why there was an arrow painted on the ceiling. Dad told us that the arrow was pointing to the direction that Muslims must face when they pray.

Dad also said, "It is good to have a gecko in your room because it eats mosquitoes and other bugs." I guess that I am okay to live with a gecko as long as it stays on the ceiling and doesn't come into my bed.

CHAPTER 6

Sea Creatures

Living down on the coast was a big change from living in the middle of the city with the horrible smells of the markets and all the people around everywhere. Our new home was pretty cool. There were lots of animals around the place, and I love animals! My favorite pet was a sheep named Louie. He just walked around everywhere, and I loved to feed him. Sometimes he chased me because he wanted me to feed him more food. There were also dogs and cats everywhere. The hotel owners, Peter and Lisa, live in an apartment below the only restaurant in town. They were very nice and treated everyone like family. Although this place was nothing like home in America, it felt like home.

I enjoyed being out of the madness of the city with all the weird smells. This place seemed much safer than the middle of the city, and I noticed that my parents didn't watch Zak and me as closely. My parents had told us that we always had to stay together in Borneo and watch out for each other. But here, we just wandered around on our own. Our favorite person to go see was a waiter named Kam CD. He would give Zak and me whatever we wanted, and we could go hang out at the restaurant by ourselves. Kam CD always made Zak his favorite drink—iced Milo. It is sort of like chocolate milk.

One of the funny things about life in Borneo was that we went barefoot everywhere. In America, you are supposed to wear shoes into a restaurant or public place, but, in Borneo, you are supposed to take your shoes off and go barefoot in restaurants and most places. I loved not having to wear shoes, because I prefer to go barefoot all the time.

One day, we hired a boat to take us out to the islands to go snorkeling and fishing. Our boat was an old catamaran named the *Fat Cat,* and the boat captains were two of the local guys that hung out around our place. The *Fat Cat* headed out to sea; there were hundreds of tiny little islands everywhere. The islands around Borneo are amazing. Some of the islands didn't have any people living on them. Dad told us that the very first *Survivor* TV show was filmed on one of the little islands near us. I did not want to be stuck on one of those islands with no food!

After sailing for about an hour, we stopped the boat and put on our snorkeling gear. I *love* to snorkel! I was the first person to jump into the water.

There were lots of fish everywhere! It was really cool to see all the different fish, but something on top of the sea kept stinging us. It felt like a little pinch that stung my skin. I asked the boat captain, "What keeps stinging me?"

He said, "Those are just jellyfish bugs." I had seen jellyfish on the beach in Florida, but I had never heard of jellyfish bugs! He told us that they are little bugs that hang out on the top of the water and sting people when they swim. The pain went away after a few minutes, but I screamed every single time they stung me. I told my mom that we were having some serious bug issues on this trip!

After snorkeling, we went to a deserted island to fish, explore, and have a picnic. While we explored the island, the Malaysian guys cooked a great dinner by fire on the beach. Zak and Dad tried to fish, and Mom and I walked around the island. When we were eating our awesome dinner, Mom went to swim some laps in a big shallow rocky area. She usually runs every day at home, but she hadn't been able to run much in Borneo. This was her plan to get in her daily exercise.

She swam about twenty minutes and then came back to the boat with her finger bleeding and this black spike in her finger. The Malaysian guys asked her, "What happened?"

She said, "My hand hit one of those black spiky sea critters with eyes, called sea urchins."

I had seen some of those sea urchins when I was snorkeling, and they look really scary. They are black balls with yellow eyes and long black spikes coming out of them. When I was snorkeling, my dad told me that they are poisonous and not to touch them. The boat captain got a serious look on his face and said to Mom, "We need to get back home and take you to the hospital."

I got really scared. I hate hospitals, and I was afraid that Mom was going to be really sick and have to stay in the hospital. Mom held my hand and said, "Everything will be okay. It is just a little sting, and it doesn't even hurt very much."

I was glad she said that, but I thought that she was just trying to make me feel better. Mom always tries to calm me down when I get upset and I think that everyone is going to die or something awful is going to happen. My family thinks that I am a little "overdramatic," but I happen to believe that I am the only one in this family that thinks logically about the dangers in life!

When we got back to the place we were living, Irene and a local girl took my mom to the doctor. It seemed like they were gone forever! When my mom came back, she said that everything was okay. The doctor got the spike out of her finger with a needle, and then gave her an antibiotic to take for five days to keep her from getting sick. Mom said that she didn't even feel sick or anything. I am never touching those black spiky critters with the funny eyes! I decided to add "poisonous fish" to my fear list.

CHAPTER 7

Everyone Was Muslim

My parents bonded with another man from Borneo named Peter (this must be a common name for men in Borneo), and he invited our family to go white-water rafting and picnicking with families from his work. My mom said that it would be a great opportunity for us to get to know the locals. Zak and I had never been white-water rafting, so we were very excited to go. Mom and Dad had been white-water rafting down the Zambezi River in Africa, so they knew what to expect. They told us that it was the dry season, as opposed to the wet season (when it rains a lot and the rivers are very full), so it would not be very dangerous to go down the river at this time of the year.

We had to get up very early in the morning to catch a bus to the river. We got on our bathing suits and river shoes and packed our gear for the day. The bus ride was about an hour long and very scary. It was up a winding mountain, and the bus was too big for the road. The road was so narrow that cars had to pull over to the side so that the bus could get by. It felt like the bus was going to fall off the side of the mountain at each curve. My mom tried to get me to sleep, but who can sleep when they might *die* from a bus crash! The bus ride seemed to take forever.

We finally arrived at the river and were greeted by a large group of people. The women and girls had on their traditional headscarves and long pants and the men had on shorts and t-shirts. They welcomed us into their group and seemed very excited for us to be joining them. They treated us like special guests and wanted to take lots of pictures of our family. Mom and I looked really out of place, because we had on our bathing suits, but all the other women and girls had on long pants, long-sleeved shirts, and headscarves. It seemed odd that they would be going into the river with long pants on instead of a bathing suit. Mom and I felt a little embarrassed, but everyone seemed to not mind that we were dressed so differently. Zak and Dad were dressed a lot like the men, so they fit in okay. Before we started our rafting trip, everyone gathered together for a Muslim prayer. We didn't understand it because they didn't say it in English, but we just stood with everyone and tried our best to participate. I liked learning how the Muslims did things differently from us.

There were about ten rafting boats in our group. The river was very cold and ran through the middle of a mountain. Mom and I were in a boat with three men and one boy. Zak and Dad were in another boat with four men. Our boat was really fun. We splashed the other boats and tried to beat Dad and Zak's boat. We had a big splash war with Zak's boat, but we won. When we went down the first rapid, I bounced out of the boat and into the cold water. It was really funny and not at all scary. Luckily, I am a really good swimmer and not afraid of the water. The men were a bit concerned because I was so young, but I didn't have any problems rafting. We stopped along the river to feed the fish right out of our hands. It tickled when the fish got the food, and I screamed really loud. Paddling the boat was very tiring, but we stopped for swim breaks. It took us about three hours to raft down the river.

After we took the rafts out, we jumped into the back of someone's truck to go to the picnic site. It must not be illegal for kids to ride in the back of a truck in Borneo. It was our family and a bunch of men in the back of the truck. The ride in the truck was just as scary as the bus ride. The driver went really fast around the curves, and he even passed several cars on the narrow road. I could tell that Mom and Dad were a bit nervous about the truck driver. Fortunately, the ride was quite short, and we arrived safely.

Everyone met at a picnic area, which was along the riverbank. We changed out of our bathing suits into our shorts. Mom said that she wished we had packed some pants to be dressed more like the Muslim women, but shorts were all we had in our backpacks. I guess shorts were better than our bathing suits! The other people made us feel very welcome in their group. They told us that the rest of the day was for eating and playing games.

The food was a buffet of rice, curry, and fruit. The food was delicious, and Dad and I tried everything. Mom and Zak are a bit picky when it comes to food, but Zak found some sweet rice wrapped in a big banana leaf that he really liked. He also loved this funky thing that looked like a huge mushroom but tasted like a sweet cake. My mom ate the rice and fruit. We never seem to find much vegetarian food for mom to eat.

After everyone finished eating, it was time for the traditional games. The highlight of the day was the games. The first thing that Dad and I did was zip-lining across the river. We climbed up this big bamboo tower with hundreds of steps. When we got to the top, a man put a harness around our legs and waist. There was a long steel cable going across the river about 200 feet above the river. The man attached my harness to the cable and told me to jump off the tower. I had zip-lined several times in Belize and Mexico, so I was just a little scared this time. I am scared of high places, so I didn't look down at the ground. I jumped off the tower and went flying really fast across the river. It was so much fun. Then, my Dad did it next. He screamed really loud as he flew across the river. We then got to zip-line back across to the other side. It was so much fun!

The next game was a rope-jumping game. Two people held a rope, and all the other people had to jump over the string without falling. Each time a person made it over the rope, it was gradually raised higher and higher. I tried to do it, but I didn't get very high. Some people could jump over the rope when it was held higher than people's heads. I'm not sure how they managed to jump that high. Then I played the stilt-walking game with stilts made out of bamboo. This was really hard. I could only go a few steps without falling. I met a local girl about my age, and we played together on the stilts. It was hard for both of us.

Zak and Dad played a game called tekro. It involves a ball about the size of a very small soccer ball, made out of rattan. The object of the game was to see how many times you could keep it up in the air with your feet, like juggling a soccer ball. All the Muslim men had a turn, and the high score was 27. Dad had a turn, and he juggled 16. Then, Zak had a turn, and he juggled 36! I knew he would do well because he is really good at juggling the soccer ball. Everyone was amazed at how good Zak was at tekro. They had never seen a kid do that well in tekro, and they started calling him "Beckham."

The next game was World Cup Soccer, but everyone had to dress in traditional outfits. This was so funny, because the traditional dress was a long skirt. People were assigned a team, and Zak and Dad were put on Sweden. Before they played, they had to put on a sarong skirt. Zak and Dad looked so funny in sarong skirts! One of the Muslim women, Harni, had to help Zak tie his sarong, but he was so skinny that his skirt kept falling off. He had to kick the ball and run while holding his skirt. Dad and Zak were really good in the World Cup Soccer. Their team didn't win the championship, but Zak got the Golden Boot Award for being the best soccer player out of everyone. He was better than all the men.

This day was one of our best days in Borneo. It was so cool to be with the Muslim families and learn about what they do for fun. We were exhausted after the long day of rafting and playing games. I was not looking forward to the bus ride down the mountain, but I was so tired that I got on the bus and slept all the way down.

CHAPTER 8

Living in a Tree House

After staying a few weeks around Kota Kinabalu, my parents told us that it was time for us to go see the other side of Borneo. Zak and I were excited to see more of Borneo, and I was hoping that maybe we could finally stay in a really nice hotel. Mom told us that we were going to have a few weeks of "hard" traveling, but I wasn't exactly sure what "hard" traveling meant.

We said good-bye to Kota Kinabalu and our new friends, and we headed to the airport for our flight to Sandakan. The flight was only about an hour, and we arrived at this tiny little airport. The plane parked on the runaway, and we had to get out and walk into this little building. It only had one baggage claim ramp. It was the smallest airport that I had ever seen.

I watched out the window as we landed, but I didn't see any signs of a city. I didn't see any buildings or any houses, only a few huts and lots of trees. I was beginning to realize that hard traveling did *not* include a nice, fancy hotel! We got our bags and jumped into a taxi with a driver that did not speak any English. Mom and Dad were trying to explain where we wanted to go, but they had trouble pronouncing the name of the place. Finally, we showed him the address in Malay, which is their language, and he seemed to understand.

We drove for about twenty minutes, and I did not see any hotels or restaurants. I wondered where we could be going and hoped to see signs of a city very soon. We finally arrived at a gravel road and began to climb up the side of the mountain. A few minutes later, the taxi stopped at this little hut and told us to get out. We got out of the taxi, took off our shoes, and walked into a hut built over on the side of the jungle. It was about the size of the deck on the back of our house in America, and it had a little roof on the top. Mom talked with a young local guy, who said that he had a place for us to stay. He seemed really nice and gave us all a cup of tea and cookies. Zak and I looked at each other with that funny look when we are not exactly sure what our parents have gotten us into.

The local guy helped us carry our bags to our hut. Our hut was a *tree house* built on the side of the jungle. It was a one-room wooden hut with a double bed and bunk beds that were equipped with mosquito nets. I had never slept under a mosquito net, but I was very thankful to have something to keep off the bugs and mosquitoes.

One wall of the tree house slid open to a little balcony hanging over the jungle. The drop from the balcony was very, very far. It made me nervous to lean on the railing. It was like we were in the top of the trees. The bathroom in the tree house was outside, so when we went to the bathroom or took a shower, the roof was open to the trees. It was definitely not the really nice hotel that I was expecting, but it was pretty cool. I had never lived in a real tree house before!

My parents said that this was a typical backpacking place and reminded them of when they were hippie backpackers. There was no TV, so everyone hung out on the balcony of the main hut that we found when we first arrived. We ate our food sitting on pillows on the floor around a wooden table. It had a tiny kitchen in the back of the hut, and we had to eat whatever they happened to be fixing on that day. It was usually rice and some type of fish or curry. We spent our evenings playing a card game called BS. One of the funny things about traveling with no TV or electronics was that our family did things that we never did at home. We never sat around together and played cards together at home, but we did this all the time in Borneo. It was kind of fun just playing cards with Mom, Dad, and Zak, even if we did fight sometimes about who won the game.

I loved watching the backpackers come and go. We never saw anyone else from America in Borneo, but there were people from Australia, England, Germany, France, Holland, and other countries. They all looked about the ages of my Uncle Robbie and Uncle Andy, which is about twenty something. We were the only family in most places, and we almost never saw any other kids. The hippie backpackers were really nice and told us stories about where they had been and how long they had been traveling. We met this really pretty girl from Belgium, who told us all about her year of traveling. Many of the people we met had been traveling for months or even a year. Mom and Dad told us that they traveled like this for years before they had Zak and me, but it was hard to imagine Mom and Dad as hippie backpackers. I wondered if Zak and I would ever be backpackers like Mom and Dad. I think I would want Mom and Dad to go with me if I decided to travel for a year!

One morning we were sitting on the pillows in the floor of the main hut, playing cards, and I spotted a really big ugly thing climbing on the wall. I screamed, "Zak, *look!*" He and the local guy went to see it, and they told me that it was a centipede and very dangerous. Okay, that was it! I jumped on the table to get my feet off the floor. The centipede began crawling on the floor toward our pillows. Everyone jumped on top of the table until the centipede disappeared through a crack in the floor. I liked this whole living in a tree house thing, but I did not like centipedes crawling where I was sitting! We also saw a big snake crawling across the path on the way back to our tree house. My dad said that this was just all part of living in the jungle.

My parents told us that everyone who comes to Borneo has to see the orangutans. Apparently, Borneo is one of the only places in the world that orangutans live. I was very excited about seeing the orangutans, and I assumed we were going to some type of zoo. We arrived at this place with a warning sign that read: DO NOT TO CARRY BACKPACKS OR PURSES BECAUSE THE ORANGUTANS WILL GET THEM. I thought this was a bit odd for a zoo, but I didn't ask any questions about it. We walked across this wooden path leading into the jungle, and I saw some monkeys in a tree. We walked a bit further and there were more monkeys and orangutans. The baby monkeys were so cute, holding onto their moms' bellies. They were swinging from vines and ropes and jumping from tree to tree.

The weird thing was that there were no cages like in a zoo. The animals could come as close as they wanted to us, but we had been warned not to touch them. The local guy told us that the orangutans and monkeys were free to come and go as they pleased. They provided food for them to eat and helped them as needed, but there were no fences to keep them here. As we were walking down the path, Zak yelled, *"Move, Ali!"* I turned around and an orangutan was walking right beside me. I stepped aside so he could get around me. Then another orangutan walked right by Zak. It was like they were following us and walking back and forth past us. I could have reached out and touched the cute little orangutan (well, not so little), but I knew that was against the rules. It was much more fun to be there with the orangutans and monkeys than in a zoo, where the animals were all in cages. I spent the next several days trying to talk my parents into letting me have a pet monkey or orangutan to take home with me to America! I thought it would be the coolest thing *ever* to have a pet orangutan!

CHAPTER 9

Jungle River Safari

After several days of living in the tree house, my parents told us that we were heading for a jungle safari. After seeing centipedes, snakes, monkeys, and orangutans, I thought we were already on a jungle safari. It was really hot and humid in the jungle already, so Zak and I were a little unsure about this jungle safari idea. Mom and Dad reassured us that we had to get through more of the jungle to get over to the islands for some time at the beach. Zak and I were looking forward to playing on the beach!

After we had breakfast on our pillows on the floor at the tree house place, a man named Rossman pulled up in a small truck to take us on a jungle safari. Rossman was a friend of one of the guys that worked at the tree house place. Dad threw our bags in the back of his truck, and we all hopped in. Dad got in the front with Rossman, and Mom, Zak, and I squeezed in the backseat of the truck. It was small and cramped, but I was very thankful to be in a truck with air conditioning! Rossman told us that it would take us several hours to get to the river. The roads were really bumpy. I tried to sleep, but every time that I fell asleep we would hit a huge bump. We stopped on the side of the road and ate lunch with the locals. It was rice and curry, again. We had been eating rice and curry for days now, and Zak had hardly eaten anything. I could tell that Mom was really worried about Zak not getting enough food to eat. I was so glad that I love rice!

Since we couldn't sleep, we just talked to Rossman. He was a Muslim and told us lots about the ways of the local people. All over Borneo, we could hear the mosque bells ring loudly to let people know that it was time to pray. They had to do a lot of praying in Borneo! Rossman told us lots about their culture. He taught us about the war and headhunters in Borneo. His uncle had actually chopped off the heads of some people. I had never been around an actual person who knew a headhunter. I asked him if there were still headhunters in Borneo, and he said, "No, not anymore." Thank goodness; I did not want to be hanging out with any headhunters on this trip!

We finally arrived in this little tiny village in the middle of nowhere. There was nothing except a few shacks along a river. We stopped at a little building, and Rossman instructed us to get out. He talked to someone in Malay, and then they showed us to our room. It was a tiny room with two small beds, and it had a weird smell.

Zak said, "Okay, this is definitely the worst place we have stayed. It is N-A-S-T-Y, nasty." We all laughed and had to agree.

Mom, always the optimist, said, "Yeah, but we can do anything for one night. We can just sleep in our sleeping bags and make pillows out of our clothes."

Dad said that he just hoped for no bedbugs. At this point, I had completely given up any hope for my five-star resort hotel.

Rossman instructed us to meet him in about an hour at this old, broken dock on the river. He picked us up in a little boat and took us down the river. I asked if there were sharks in the river, and he said, "No, just crocodiles!" I don't like sharks or crocodiles, but he told me that the crocs only came out at night. We spotted lots of long-tailed macaque monkeys and proboscis monkeys (they are the ones with really big noses) in the trees. Entire families of monkeys were hanging out together in the trees right above our boat. We spotted all types of birds and big lizards. Zak was really good at spotting animals, and Rossman would say, "Good spot, Zak!" My favorite animals to see were the monkeys with the big noses. I spent the entire boat trip trying to once again convince my parents to let me have a baby monkey to keep at our house, but they were not very thrilled with the idea.

After our afternoon boat trip, we went back for a quick dinner of rice and curry before our night jungle safari. I was a little nervous about a night jungle safari to hunt for crocodiles.

I know that my family thinks that I can be a drama queen, but I had to point out to everyone that our boat was not very big to be hunting for crocodiles at night! Our little tin fishing boat at home was bigger than Rossman's boat. Dad said, "Ali, it will be fine," but I didn't believe him.

After dinner, Rossman picked us up in his little boat. It was just Rossman and our family, sailing into the dark night on a little boat to look for crocodiles. I told my mom that I was not good with this at all, and I held on tightly to her hand! To make matters worse, the boat did not have any lights. We only had a small flashlight, and Dad brought two little lights that go on your head.

It was pitch black on the river, and big logs kept hitting our little boat. I was certain that our boat was going to tip over and we were all going to be eaten by crocodiles! We first spotted a big cliff of rocks with birds that looked like a huge family of bats. It was difficult to see because it was so pitch black. I would have felt more comfortable if there were other travelers around and not just our crazy family on this tiny boat with no lights!

We floated for about an hour down these little, scary creeks, heading away from the main river. We saw an owl and several types of weird, scary cat things that looked like they were from Africa, but we never saw a crocodile. It was scary enough just knowing that the river was full of crocodiles swimming near us. Rossman told us that they were hiding all around us but that it was difficult to spot their eyes peering up in the water. Zak was disappointed, but I was thrilled to have missed seeing a crocodile, especially in our little boat. If a crocodile had attacked us, I am pretty sure the crocodile would have won!

We said goodnight to Rossman and thanked him for the boat trip. We played a few family card games of BS outside in the lights before going to our room for the night. The room somehow looked worse after dark. I saw a gecko on the wall and hoped it would eat all the bugs that I was sure would crawl on me in the night. We got out our sleeping bags and made pillows out of our backpacks and clothes. Luckily, we were all very tired and went to sleep quickly. It is surprising that when you are tired, you really can sleep just about anywhere! I dreamt of falling out of our little boat and being eaten by crocodiles. I decided to add crocodile hunting in a tiny boat at night to my fear list!

CHAPTER 10

The Worst Day EVER

Our next destination was the island of Mabul for some diving, snorkeling, and beach time. But first, we had to get there, which is often a challenge in Borneo. I learned that getting to places in Borneo was not as easy as at home, and everywhere required at least a day of traveling. Rossman agreed to drive us in his truck to Semporna, which was about three hours from the river. A three-hour drive in Borneo meant a very long, bumpy ride, because the roads are narrow and not very good. There are no interstates like we have in America, and sometimes the roads had collapsed, which made it very difficult for cars and buses. Rossman helped pass the time by telling us more stories about headhunters and his family.

Semporna is a small fishing village with local fishermen everywhere. All the local huts were built on stilts over the water. There must have been thousands of people living in these water villages. It was a maze that

I could have gotten lost in for days! Mom said that we had to spend one night in Semporna to catch the boat to Mabul early the next day. Rossman found us the best place to stay in town, which wasn't a five-star hotel, but was okay, compared to the other places we had stayed. It was a hotel with a restaurant. Our hotel room window overlooked all the fishing boats and the market. Fishing boats were constantly bringing in their fish and going back to sea. Zak, Dad, and I loved to watch the boats bring in their fish. They would throw hundreds of fish onto the dock right below our window. We opened our window and could smell all the fish just below us. It was really cool.

The morning that we had to catch the boat to the island was a big rush for us. We had to pack our bags, eat breakfast, walk about ten minutes to the ferry, and catch the boat by 8:00 a.m. Zak and I always complained when we had to get up early and rush in the mornings. Mom woke us up and said, "Get ready and come eat breakfast before the boat ride to the island." Mom took the bags down and planned to meet us at breakfast.

Right when she left, I decided that I would go with her instead of staying with Dad and Zak. I ran after her, but the elevator door closed behind her before she saw me coming. We were on the fifth floor, so I decided to run down the stairwell to meet her. I got in the stairwell and started running down the steps, but I could not tell how many floors I had gone down. When I tried to get out one of the doors, it was locked. I went down another floor and it was locked. I tried another floor, but it was locked too. I began to panic when I realized that I was alone in this yucky, hot, scary stairwell. I ran back up to where I came in and that door was locked too. I tried every single door, and they were all locked!

I was very panicked and scared. I began to beat the doors and scream, "I am a nine-year-old girl from America and I'm locked in here! *Please help me! Someone please help me!*" I screamed over and over, and I beat the doors until my hands were red. I even tried to go the ground floor, which I knew would open up to all those fishing boats. I thought if I could just get out, I could run around the outside of the hotel by myself and come in the front door. I planned to run really fast so nobody could kidnap me. It didn't seem like a very good choice, but I couldn't think of any other choices. My plan was crushed when the ground floor door was locked too!

I ran back up a few floors screaming over and over, "*Help me!* I'm a nine-year-old girl from America and I'm locked in here! *Help me please!*" Then I saw a window and tried to pull myself up the window, but I wasn't strong enough! My hands were black from trying to pull myself up. I continued to scream, but it seemed hopeless. I ran up and down the stairs again, banging and screaming on every floor. I had been stuck in the stairwell for what seemed like forever. I was crying and afraid that I would never get out, or that someone would find me and kidnap me. It was the worst feeling in the world. I wanted my mom so badly! Screaming and beating the door seemed to be my only hope, even if the person who found me was a mean person. Being found by anyone was better than being left alone in here forever!

After what seemed like forever, a Muslim woman heard my screams and opened the door. I was crying and said, "I am a nine-year-old American girl, and I was locked in the stairwell."

She asked me, "Where is your room?"

I answered, "My mom is at breakfast, and I need to find my mom!" We got on the elevator together and it stopped at a random floor. When the elevator opened, there was Zak, looking for me. I fell into his arms, crying, and he hugged me as the Muslim lady took us to the lobby. When the elevator opened, Mom was in the lobby, crying. She held me, cried like I had never seen her cry before, and then she threw up in a garbage can. She was shaking because she thought that I had been kidnapped. They had been searching for me for about thirty minutes. She had screamed all around the hotel that her daughter was missing and begged people to please help find me. But everyone just looked at my mom and didn't understand what was happening. My mom felt so helpless and scared.

It was weird because, just a few days earlier, we had been talking about Maddie, a little English girl that had been kidnapped while her family was on vacation in another country. They never found Maddie and still have no clue what really happened to her. I asked my mom if she had been thinking of Maddie, and she just cried and nodded her head yes. I was so happy to be back with my mom, and I held on to her so tight. None of us could eat any breakfast. It was the worst experience of my life, and it wasn't even 8:00 in the morning yet! Stairwells just went to the top of my fear list! I sure do hope that

Maddie is okay and that they find her someday like they found me.

CHAPTER 11

The Island of Children

Despite our morning drama, we caught the early morning boat to Mabul Island. It was a pretty small boat, and the ride took about an hour. When the boat got close to the island, I saw fancy huts built on stilts out into the sea, like I had seen on TV and in travel magazines. They looked like little houses floating in the sea, connected by bridges across the sea. I asked Mom and Dad, "Do we get to stay in those fancy huts on the water?"

But, they just laughed and said, "Those places are *very* expensive and we don't have enough money to stay there."

I bet those places have free little shampoos and a mini-bar with good snacks! Mom reminded me that we are more on a "backpacker" budget than an "expensive holiday" budget. I just crossed my fingers and hoped that our backpacker budget included somewhere nice to stay on the island with a real bed and no bedbugs!

When we got to the island, it was amazing. The boat pulled up to a long pier, and we could see lots of colorful fish swimming everywhere. The sea was very clear and bright blue. We got our bags off the boat and walked down the long pier. It was odd, because on one side of the pier there were really expensive floating huts for the rich tourists, but on the other side of the pier there was a local village with tiny shack huts that the poor people lived in.

I was shocked at how poor the people were on the island. I had never seen people so poor in my life. It was so different from anything I had ever seen in America, or even on television. There were children running around everywhere, naked, or with only rags for clothes. Their huts were about the size of the playhouses that you see in kids' backyards in America. There were also cats running around everywhere. I remembered that the doctor in America told us not to touch animals in Borneo because they might have diseases. I really wanted to pick up one of the cats, but I thought that it wasn't such a good idea. The children just stared at us and waved as we walked down the pier. Zak and I waved at the children and followed Mom and Dad. We had no idea where we were going.

Surprisingly, we were staying in a really cool hut right on the beach. My favorite part was the hammock on the balcony! It might not have been as cool as those expensive floating huts, but it was better than the huts of the poor children and it was perfect for our family. After we got our stuff put away in our hut, we decided to go exploring and walk around the island.

It took only about thirty minutes to walk around the entire island. We walked through the local villages, and there were kids everywhere. The kids were playing in puddles of water and some were naked. They would run up to Zak and me and want to touch us or just watch us. The kids seemed to be playing soccer with plastic water bottles and playing chase with each other. Some of the kids had swollen bellies like I had seen on those TV commercials about adopting children in Africa. My mom told me that happened because the children didn't get enough proper food to eat. We also noticed that the children would just take a poop in the sand right by the sea, and then jump in the sea to clean themselves. They didn't have any real bathroom, and I don't know if they even had clean water.

There were hundreds of little kids running around everywhere, but very few adults or teenagers. The few adults that we saw were really old grandmas that were repairing fishing nets, making jewelry, or cooking rice. The kids had little groups, with the leaders being about the same ages as Zak and me. The kids did not go to school and seemed to take care of each other.

The people that owned our hut told us that most of the people living on the island were children who came to the island illegally from other countries around Borneo. After coming to the island, their parents were usually caught and were sent back to their home countries, or they moved to the main part of Borneo to work and get money. The parents just left the kids on the island to have a better life. When the kids get to be teenagers, they leave the island to go find work too. This was really hard for me to understand, because I could not imagine life being better without my parents.

Zak and I noticed that the kids seemed to be having a great time. They didn't go to school, so they were always playing games, chasing each other and laughing. While we were living on the island, Zak and I played games with the kids. Zak taught them how to juggle a soccer ball, and we played soccer with the kids. The kids loved to play with us. We also showed them pictures on our iPhone of America and our friends at home. The kids loved seeing pictures of us in our soccer uniforms playing soccer in America. I felt famous when all the kids were looking at my pictures and wanted to follow me. They also loved seeing pictures of snow, because they had never seen snow before. We tried to teach the kids some words in English. Mom was really good at teaching the kids colors and numbers with funny songs. They would repeat everything that she said.

Before we left America, we collected soccer jerseys from our travel soccer teams to take to the poor people in Borneo. My mom said that it was important that we give something to the people in Borneo to try to help them. I was not happy about putting extra stuff in my bag when I was packing in America, but the kids absolutely loved the soccer shirts! It was so awesome to see them run around in their new shirts. I guess Mom was right after all! Those shirts were more important than my flip-flops.

It was hard for me to see all the poor children on the island, especially the little babies. I really wanted to take a baby home with me and take care of her forever! I begged my mom and dad to please let me have a baby. I promised to be the best big sister *EVER* and do all the work to take care of the baby.

My mom hugged me and said, "Ali, you would be a great big sister, but we are not allowed to take a baby home with us." She tried to explain stuff about international adoptions, but none of it made any sense to me. I just wanted to take a baby home and love her forever! I will never forget the kids on Mabul Island! I think of them often and cross my fingers that they are still playing, laughing, and wearing the soccer jerseys.

CHAPTER 12

Underwater Life

The reason that we went to Mabul Island was because it is one of the best diving and snorkeling places in the entire world. My mom and dad have been diving at lots of places, like the Great Barrier Reef in Australia, and they are both certified divers. But this was a new experience for Zak and me. We saw lots of colorful fish swimming in the sea by just looking off the pier, so we were very excited about learning to scuba dive!

Zak and I are both really good swimmers, and we have done lots of snorkeling. However, before we could scuba dive, we had to pass a few tests. Our dive instructors were Liz from England and Tyce from Holland. Zak and Dad were on a team with Tyce, and Mom and I were on a team with Liz. It is called the "buddy system," because you always have to have a buddy when you go diving in the ocean. We had to use the buddy system a lot in Borneo. Dad told us, "If you don't watch out for your buddy, they could get lost or really hurt." I was really glad that Mom was my buddy instead of Zak. I wanted to make sure that my buddy was always watching me, and I didn't really trust Zak for that job!

Liz and Tyce gave us a safety talk and showed us a few hand signals to use underwater to talk to each other. I liked learning sign language! Then, we got on our wet suits, air tanks, masks, and flippers. It was so hard to walk with all that heavy gear on my back, but it felt fine as soon as I jumped into the sea. Once we got into the sea, Zak and I had to pass three tests before we could dive. First, we had to put the regulator into our mouth and breathe underwater. The regulator is the mouthpiece that connects to the air tanks. It looked like a big hose coming out of our mouths. It was really cool to be able to breathe underwater, but then our instructors made us take out our regulator in the water and put it back in our months. Zak and I were really good at that test and passed on the first try. Our next test was to equalize our ear pressure, like you do when you are on a plane and your ears start to hurt. We had to pinch our noses closed under water and blow really hard. You have to do this over and over when you go into really deep water, or your ears will feel like they are going to explode. Zak and I passed this test with no problem too. We were good at popping our ears after all the flights that we had been on lately.

The final test was the hardest. We had to go underwater, take our masks off, put them back on and then blow all the water out of the masks. I hated doing this, because the salt water got in my eyes and nose. I had to try this several times before I could manage to do it under the water. Zak had a hard time with this test too, but after several tries we passed the final test and were ready for scuba diving.

Because of our ages, Zak and I were only allowed to dive down twelve meters, or about forty feet deep. We rode out to sea for about twenty minutes in a little boat and then stopped on a coral reef. As we were riding in the boat, I asked Liz, "Will there be any sharks out here?"

She said, "Maybe, but they won't hurt you." That was not exactly what I wanted to hear. Sharks are also on my fear list. Ever since I watched the movie *Soul Surfer* and the girl got her arm eaten off by a shark, I have not been okay with swimming with sharks! I did not like the thought of swimming with any sharks, even if they were supposed to be "nice" sharks!

When the boat stopped, Liz told us to do a backward flip off the boat while holding our masks on our faces. This was really scary, and it felt like I was going to hit the boat. Luckily, I am very good at doing back flips on my trampoline at home, so I just pretended that I was on the trampoline and rolled backward off the side of the boat. I went first, and then Zak followed me.

Once we all got in the water and gave the "okay" sign, we started going down deep into the water. I had to equalize the pressure lots to keep my ears from hurting. We went down so deep that I couldn't even see the sky when I looked up. I felt like a mermaid. I was amazed as we swam with schools of hundreds of bright, colorful fish. It was like swimming in a huge aquarium with thousands of fish! The fish had such bright colors, and I swam in the middle of them. We saw starfish, a weird-looking sea snake creature, giant clams, and a lionfish that really looked like a fish that had a lion's head! Zak also spotted a stingray in the sand and showed it to me. I was really scared, because I remembered that a stingray is what killed Steve Irwin, the famous man from Australia, the Crocodile Hunter.

We also saw gigantic loggerhead turtles! The turtles were bigger than Zak and me! I had never seen turtles this huge in my entire life. Zak and I swam right beside them, and they didn't even seem to care that we were so close that we could touch them. But we didn't touch them, because you are not supposed to touch any of the wildlife or coral when diving or snorkeling.

As we were diving and looking at all the fish, we noticed that Dad was missing. Tyce had a really cool white board and marker that could write underwater. He wrote a note to Liz and my mom that said, "Where is Steve?" I saw the note and began to get scared. I looked around and Dad was gone. He then wrote another note to us all that said, "Cyn ←→ Zak. Liz ←→ Ali. Find Steve." I knew the note meant that Mom needed to buddy with Zak while Liz watched me. Tyce swam off and left us way down deep in the ocean.

Mom looked at me and gave me the "okay" sign and the "I love you" sign in sign language. These were the only things I knew in sign language. I hated not being able to talk to her, but I knew what she was trying to tell me. The worst part about scuba diving was not being able to talk to each other. We swam through lots of fish, but I didn't care about the fish. I was just worried about my daddy being eaten by a shark or getting lost in the ocean. I kept looking to see if I could find him.

After what seemed like forever, Dad and Tyce swam back to us. I'm not sure how they found us so deep in the ocean, because it was really dark, but I was *very* happy to see my daddy! When we came up to the top of the water, Dad said that he started following a big turtle to take some photos with his underwater camera and then got lost from us. I knew it was not a good idea to be a buddy with Zak or Dad! I decided to always have Mom on the buddy system.

During our stay on Mabul Island, we went on lots of diving and snorkeling adventures. Zak and I got really good at diving and snorkeling. Zak liked snorkeling the best, and I liked diving the best. With each dive and snorkel, we saw different things, as we explored the sea. Luckily, we never saw any sharks. It was one of the coolest things ever! I think that I might be a dive instructor some day. I think that would be a really cool job, except for the shark part!

CHAPTER 13

Sleepover with the Locals

Our next stop on this family adventure was the northwest side of Borneo, in a place called Sarawak. Borneo is much bigger than I thought, and it took a very long time to get all around this big place. Mom and Dad said, "We are going to Sarawak to live with the locals and go trekking through the jungle." Zak and I just gave each other one of those looks, like we were not really sure about this plan. Obviously, this was not going to include a really nice hotel!

The night before we headed into the jungle, we found a great little Indian restaurant. Zak was so excited because he had not been eating much, since the only food we had lately was rice and local foods. Mom and Zak were both losing weight on this trip from not eating very much. I don't think it is good to be a vegetarian in Borneo or to be a picky eater like Zak. Dad and I are really good at eating everything! The Indian food was awesome!

Zak said, "I feel sick from eating so much."

Dad replied, "Well, hopefully that will keep us full for the next several days when we are going to be in the jungle." Zak and I hoped that he was just kidding.

The next morning, a man named Mr. Tam picked us up in his truck for the two-hour drive into the jungle to the Annah Rais Longhouse. We threw our bags in the back of the truck and all jumped in. As we drove, I noticed that there were no hotels or anything around us. We were really driving into nowhere. We finally stopped at this tiny little village with a small field and soccer goal made out of bamboo. The place was very quiet, with lots of huts connected by a long wooden walkway.

We carried our bags up to a little wooden hut, and out came a local man named Mr. Edwards. He was a big man with a chubby belly. He smiled all the time and reminded me of Buddha or Santa Claus. We all liked him instantly. He gave us some water to drink and welcomed us to his home. He told us that the people in the longhouses are all one tribe from Borneo living together, and that they live a lot like the way that they lived hundreds of years ago. I looked around and noticed that there were no hotels or buildings anywhere around us, just one long wooden walkway connecting lots of little wooden huts or shacks. I wondered where we were going to stay, and I knew Zak was thinking the same thing.

Then Mr. Edwards took us into his home and showed us two small bedrooms. Each room had a mattress on the floor, and there was a small bathroom outside. The bathroom had a hosepipe for us to wash ourselves, but it only had cold water. It was kind of dark and seemed a little scary. Mr. Edwards said that Zak and I could stay in one bedroom together and that Mom and Dad could stay in the other room. I did not like that idea, because I was not staying in any strange room in a strange house without a parent in clear sight, especially after getting lost in the stairwell!

Mom told me that the "girls" would sleep in one room, and the "boys" would sleep in the other room. I don't think she wanted me to be out of her sight either! It seemed a bit strange to be having a sleepover in this little wooden hut with people we didn't know, but we didn't have any other choice, because we were in the middle of nowhere, with no hotels or restaurants.

As we walked through the little hut, I noticed Mr. Edwards's family. There were some older children sitting on a couch who looked about twenty or thirty, and his wife was in a tiny kitchen, cooking rice. Mrs. Edwards brought us each a cup of tea to drink. After drinking our cups of tea, we walked around all the longhouses in the village. The village had about eighty families living in huts connected together by a bamboo bridge. As we walked around, we saw people making traditional arts and crafts. We then went into the most sacred hut in the village. Mr. Edwards explained that inside were lots of spirits, but they would do us no harm. He told us to be very quiet and respectful of the spirits. I was a little scared because I didn't want to make any spirits mad at me! When I looked up, I saw a wire cage with about ten real skulls inside! I had never seen a dead skull before, and it was very creepy. There was also a big sword that Mr. Edwards said was the actual sword that had chopped off the heads! I wanted to get out of that hut very quickly. I was not okay sleeping near people's heads that had been chopped off! My dad said that it was all part of the culture, but I still did not like the idea of dead skulls being in the hut next to us.

We spent the evenings with Mr. Edwards, who told us all sorts of stories about things that had happened to him in the days of the headhunters. Some of the stories were really scary and made me have scary dreams at night. Mr. Edwards had all this really cool stuff for Zak and me to play with. He had lots of blowguns, and Zak and I had contests to see who was the best at shooting the blow darts. Zak thought he was the best, but I was pretty good too! Mr. Edwards also had lots of big knives and machetes. Zak and Dad loved looking at all of them.

We found all kinds of traditional musical instruments and costumes. The locals taught us to play the drums and these funny bells that we hit with sticks. Zak and I got pretty good at making cool-sounding beats, but Dad was the best at this. He could play beats on the drums that sounded like songs we knew. Mom said that Dad had natural musical talent, because his family in England were musicians. Unfortunately, Mom has no musical talent at all in her family!

Life in the longhouse village was pretty cool. We ate what the locals ate and just blended in with their way of life. At first, it was a bit scary sleeping on the floor in a strange place with skulls nearby, but, as always, we just rolled with the experience. I was very thankful that my mom agreed to a "girls" room because I would have been really scared in a room without an adult!

CHAPTER 14

OMG—Leeches!

One day at the longhouses, we decided to take a hike into the rainforest to find some kind of waterfall that Mr. Edwards had told us about. He warned us that it was a pretty tough hike, but we were up for the challenge. One of the local guys, Mr. Richard, agreed to take us on the trek. Mr. Richard was an older man who lived in one of the longhouses. He was very quiet and did not look like a good hiking guide. We put on our hiking shoes and mosquito repellent and packed water bottles in our day packs. Mr. Richard also carried a day pack full of stuff. Before we set out hiking, Mr. Edwards gave each of us a big bamboo walking stick and warned us to be careful of the leeches.

I said, "Leeches?" All the adults laughed and Dad told me it would be okay and not to worry about it. I just hoped that Mr. Edwards was joking with us, but I had a funny feeling that it might not be a joke.

We started walking up the road and then Mr. Richard turned onto a tiny little path in the jungle. He then stopped and said, "You must put a piece of bamboo behind your ear, and you may no longer call anyone by their real name because it will anger the spirits and gods. You must always address each other by your spirit names. My spirit name is Light."

Our family didn't have any spirit names, so we quickly had to come up with names. I said, "I am Rock."

Zak said, "I'm Nighthawk."

We named Mom, "Stick," and Dad tried to be "Dragon," but we all called him "Dragonfly." We each put a piece of cut bamboo behind our ears. I wasn't really convinced of this whole angering the gods thing, but the jungle looked pretty scary and I didn't want to take any chances!

As we headed into the jungle, Mr. Richard took out his big machete and said, "This is my credit card because it is the only thing that can buy us anything where we are going." He told us that money was of no use in the jungle. The only thing that will help you find food or protect you is a big machete. I was not so certain this trekking in the jungle was such a good idea.

I had been hiking in parks in America, so I thought I knew what this trek was going to be like, but boy was I ever wrong. We trekked for hours and hours through the thick jungle with Mr. Richard cutting the path in front of us with his machete. We had to walk single file and climb up very steep hills and across streams. Sometimes we crossed the streams by walking over bamboo sticks. They were very slippery and hard to climb. I was very thankful to have my walking stick to help me balance.

We trekked for hours and never saw another person in the jungle. I wondered why we were all alone. Where were all the other tourists in Borneo? It seemed weird that it was only our crazy family trekking through this desolate jungle. When we did hikes in America, we saw lots of other people. But here, it was just Mr. Richard, the machete, the jungle creatures, and us. I was very glad to have Mr. Richard with the four of us. Our family could have easily gotten lost in the jungle, because there were no signs or clear trails. I tried to always hike with Dad in front of me and Mom behind me, just in case I took a wrong turn or got left behind. Zak liked to be in the front of everyone and explore things first. Sometimes it was difficult to see each other because the jungle bush was taller than me!

After hiking about three hours, we came across the most amazing waterfall that I had ever seen in my life. It reminded me of something out of a movie! It was enormous, and the waterfall sounded like a train, because it was falling from so high! It felt like we had found a lost treasure, because no one was at this amazing waterfall but us! Zak and I jumped in the water, and it was freezing cold, but felt great after the long, hot trek. Our family started climbing up the rocks to the waterfall. It had about five different levels. We were playing in the water on the lowest level when we noticed that Zak was gone. We looked around and discovered that he had managed to climb through the jungle on his own and get several levels up above us. He was really high up! Zak shouted down to us, "Y'all, come up here! It is awesome!"

Dad, Mom, and I tried to follow his path, but the jungle was really thick with vines and trees, and the path was very steep. We had to climb up tree branches and pull each other up. We ended up on a level about thirty feet up, but Zak was still about fifteen feet above us, on a high cliff. We had no idea how he got so high!

We couldn't figure out how to get to Zak, and he couldn't get back down the same way he got up, because the jungle path was too steep for him to climb back down. Mom had a foolish idea that he should jump like a monkey to a tree branch and then shimmy down the tree.

Zak said, "You really want me to jump and swing on that tree?"

Mom said, "Yeah, I think it is the only way down." It was a tall, skinny tree growing out of the waterfall from one level to the next. Zak tried to lean out and grab the tree, but it was about a foot too far out for him to grab.

Mom said, "The only way to get the tree is to leap and grab onto the tree as you jump." I was scared, just looking at how high up he was. I am very scared of heights—fear of heights has been on my fear list for years!

All of a sudden, with no warning, Zak soared off the fifteen-foot cliff and leaped to the tree. When he landed in the tree, the limb broke and started falling down. Mom and I screamed as we watched Zak and the tree falling off the cliff. I thought for sure that my brother was going to die. Luckily, the tree fell in slow motion and Zak just hung on as it was falling. He looked like a monkey flying through the air, holding onto the tree limb. When the tree hit the rocks, we heard a loud bang, but Zak landed safely right beside us. He was lucky not to get hurt!

Mom said, "Well, I guess that was not such a bright idea after all!"

After the tree drama, Zak and I started playing around in the waterfall. We were splashing around on the level about thirty feet from the bottom of the waterfall when Zak said, "I think there is something on my toe." He took off his shoes, and Mom and Dad looked at his toe and thought it was a black rock. Mom tried to hit it off and noticed that it was attached to his toe.

We all looked a bit closer, and Dad said, "OMG, that is a leech!"

Zak screamed as loud as I have ever heard him scream, *"Ahh! Help, do something, get this leech off me!!!"*

Mom and Dad looked at each other, but I had no idea what they were going to do. Dad said, "Don't pull it off because the head will get stuck inside you! You are supposed to put salt on it." This made Zak scream again! The problem was that we were thirty feet up on a ledge, and the only way down was a hard trek back through the jungle or down the slippery cliffs of the waterfall.

Dad said, "I'll run back through the jungle and bring the salt and machete back up here for Zak."

When Dad left, Zak noticed another leech on his other foot. He screamed, "OMG! I have another leech on my foot! They are all over me!"

Mom tried to use her calm voice and said, "Zak, it will be okay. We will get the leeches off you as fast as we can. Just sit still and soak your feet in the cold water, maybe it will make the leeches come off."

I was getting a little freaked out at this point. I kept looking all over my body for leeches. I was afraid that I might have leeches in my hair. My hair is really long, thick and curly, so a leech could easily hide in my hair. I quickly felt all around my hair for leeches. Next, I took off my shoes and checked my feet too. Luckily, I didn't find any leeches on me. It seemed like forever until Dad came back with the salt and big knife.

When Zak saw the knife, he screamed, "Don't hurt me!"

Mom said in her really calm voice, "Zak, it will be okay. This won't hurt, and we will have all the leeches off you in just a minute. I promise everything will be okay."

Zak sat on a rock, and Dad poured salt onto the leech and then flicked it with the knife.

When the leech came off, blood poured out of Zak's foot and out of the leech. I was amazed at how much blood there was everywhere. I asked Zak, "Does it hurt?"

He said, "No, actually it feels okay now." Dad then got the leech off his other foot, and we all watched as the blood poured out once again. I hated that Zak got leeches, but I was really thankful that it was Zak instead of me. I'm not sure that I would have been as brave as Zak!

After more playing in the waterfall, we made our way down to the bottom again. Mr. Richard had started a fire and cooked some food. He had brought a can of sardines and rice in his backpack. He cooked the sardines on the fire and cooked the rice in bamboo canes that he cut down in the jungle.

We ate the rice, sardines, and drank the rice juice from the bamboo sticks. The rice juice tasted a bit like warm sugar water. It was pretty good. Dad and I thought the rice and sardine curry was awesome, but Mom and Zak would not eat it. They did manage to eat rice and drink the bamboo water! We were all starving and needed energy to hike back through the jungle.

By the time we got back to the longhouses, it was nearly dark and we were all exhausted! I was thrilled to be back safely at the longhouses. We all checked for leeches when we got back to the longhouses. It had been an incredible day that I will remember forever. On the way out of the jungle, Mr. Richard cut weeds in the jungle with his "credit card" for Mrs. Edwards to cook us for dinner. That night we ate jungle weeds, rice, and curry. I was amazed how good the weeds tasted cooked with soy sauce. Zak was so hungry that he even ate some weeds and rice.

It was sometimes difficult for my brain to comprehend all the things that I observed and experienced in one day. It felt like an entire week of adventures packed into just one day! I went to sleep on the floor in the little hut and dreamt about leeches crawling on me. I woke up in the middle of the night and screamed, *"Mom, Mom, get them off me! They are crawling on me!"*

My mom jumped up and said, "Ali, are you okay?"

I said, "I think so, but can you please feel and make sure that I don't have any leeches crawling on me or in my hair?" She checked me for leeches once again and reassured me that I was leech free! My fear list is getting really long in Borneo!

CHAPTER 15

Hot Springs

The morning after our big trek through the jungle, we were all very tired and sore. We woke to a breakfast of fried rice, fruit, and tea that Mrs. Edwards had fixed for us. Thankfully, I can eat rice any time of the day! After breakfast, Dad decided that we should go to the natural hot springs to soak our sore muscles. He said that it would be just like getting in a hot tub at a fancy hotel, but Zak and I were doubtful about that!

There were no buses or taxis in the longhouse villages, so Dad asked some guy with a motorcycle to take us to the hot springs. He could only take two of us at a time. On the first trip, he took Dad and me on the back of his motorcycle. It was a little scary, because they didn't have any motorcycle helmets like in America. I hoped that there were no police around, because I did not like breaking the rules, especially in a foreign country! Dad put me in the middle of him and the driver. I held on tightly to the driver, and Dad held onto to me. Then, the motorcycle dude went back and picked up Mom and Zak. It was funny seeing Zak and Mom arrive on the back of the motorcycle.

After the motorcycle guy dropped us off, we walked about fifteen minutes until we saw this little creek. There was no one at the creek except our family. I was beginning to think that we must be the only people in the entire world who were spending our summer vacation in Borneo. I was certain that every place at the beach in Florida would have been packed with people on vacation!

We got in the water and it was freezing cold, but we could see steam coming off the water in different little pools of water, surrounded by natural rock walls. Dad said, "Let's go over to those rocks with the steam and feel the water."

We waded through the freezing cold water and felt inside the rock pool. I screamed, "Ouch!" because the water was extremely hot. Dad warned us not to get into the water because it would burn us. We then went to another rock pool and felt the water. This time it felt like a hot bath at home. We all jumped in and soaked in the natural hot springs. It felt great to just lie in a hot bath! Zak and I kept jumping from the hot water to the really cold water. He kept splashing me with the cold water!

As we were sitting in the hot springs, a local guy came wandering out of the jungle with his "credit card" (a machete).

He had cleared a path to walk through the jungle. He was startled to see us there, and we were startled to see a strange man standing by us with a machete. But after a minute, he just walked across the creek without saying a word to us. I don't think the locals find many American families hanging out in their hot springs. Lucky for us, the locals did not seem to mind us hanging around their village. They seemed as curious about us as we were about them. I thought the local tribe people were very nice.

After hanging out in the hot springs for about an hour, the motorcycle dude came back and transported us back to the longhouses. Dad and I went back first, and then he went to get Mom and Zak. We packed our bags, said our goodbyes to Mr. Edwards and his family, and headed back to Sarawak and civilization. Our stay at the longhouses was amazing, and the experiences that I had will be hard to forget. I don't think that I will ever stop dreaming about leeches and headhunters!

CHAPTER 16

Home

After a month of hard and adventurous traveling around Borneo, it was time for that long flight home. I was not looking forward to that very, very, very, long trip home! I think it was worse because I knew what to expect and how long it was going to take to get home. We were all very tired on the flight home, and Zak got all the good sleeping spots again! His feet were in my face the entire trip. As expected, it took forever to get home, and I didn't want to get back on another airplane for a long, long time!

When we were on the plane home, I asked everyone in my family, "What was the best part of your trip?" Everyone had a different answer.

Zak said, "Playing soccer with all the Muslims in the World Cup Soccer Game."

Mom said, "Hiking through the rainforest."

Dad said, "Living in the tree house."

And, I said, "Diving on Mabul Island and playing with the poor children." I guess it really took an entire month to fit all those different favorite things in for everyone.

When I got back home, the first thing that I did was run into my room and jump on my bed! Zak went straight to Xbox and started playing with his friends. It was great to be back home and sleep in my own bed, but I also missed things about Borneo. After living in very small spaces together for a month, our house seemed so big.

It was odd. In some ways, it seemed like I was in Borneo forever, but in other ways, it seemed like the time just flew by so quickly. Before my trip to Borneo, I had no idea what to expect, and I wasn't very excited about the so-called family adventure. It was definitely not a week at the beach in Florida! I often wonder why no one else does crazy things like our family did in Borneo. Maybe people are just afraid of trying strange things, or maybe they are afraid of things like bedbugs, leeches, or not knowing where you are going to stay at night.

My fear list got a bit longer in Borneo, and I still have scary dreams about getting lost in the stairwell and being kidnapped. But, I also have great dreams of diving in the sea, playing with lost children on the Mabul Island, playing games with the Muslim families, getting a pet orangutan, and many other exciting things.

When my friends asked me about my summer trip, I didn't really know what to say. I wanted to tell them all about it, but I also knew that they wouldn't really understand what I was talking about. It wasn't just one or two big things that we did; it was the millions of little things that we did in Borneo that made it really special. I wish that everyone could spend a summer vacation in Borneo so that they could really understand all the things that made my summer vacation an amazing adventure.

A long hike in the rainforest

Orangutan in the jungle

Life as a backpacker

The "Island of Children"

Headhunters!

Playing soccer with the children

About the Authors

Cindy Davis holds a PhD in social work and is a university professor. She has written extensively in academic journals and has published academic books. This is her first travel book and first book for children and young teens. Cindy spent several years backpacking around Southeast Asia and Africa with her partner, Steve Rollason. They have lived in Hong Kong and Australia. Their son, Zak, was born in Australia in 1999. This book is coauthored by her ten-year-old daughter, Ali Rollason. Ali enjoys soccer, gymnastics, and her horses. They currently live in Franklin, Tennessee, and travel overseas whenever possible.